Draft programme

Communist Party
of Great Britain

Published in the United Kingdom by
Communist Party of Great Britain, BCM Box 928, London WC1N 3XX
communistparty.co.uk

First edition 1995
Second edition 2011
Third edition 2023
Fourth edition 2025

ISBN 978-1-4475-8949-5

Made and printed by Lulu, www.lulu.com

Contents

Introduction

The Communist Party of Great Britain was founded on July 31 1920. Our CPGB was the British section of the Communist International and resulted from a process of communist rapprochement directly inspired by the October 1917 revolution in Russia and the example of Lenin's Bolsheviks.

Despite its early limitations and later failures, as an organisation the CPGB is undoubtedly the highest achievement of the workers' movement in Britain.

This is the draft third programme. The first programme, *For Soviet Britain*, was adopted in February 1935 at the CPGB's 13th Congress. Within the year, this left sectarian mishmash was officially deemed outdated. In 1939 a Draft programme was produced. Suffice to say, the outbreak of inter-imperialist war that year made it irrelevant.

The *British road to socialism*, the second programme, was published in draft form in 1951 and was officially adopted at the 22nd Congress in April 1952. Its underlying claim was that socialism would be achieved through transforming parliament and via a series of Labour governments.

Both previous programmes and their various revisions and editions marked successive shifts to the right by the class collaborationist factions then dominating the leadership of the CPGB. As a result Marxism was effectively replaced by Fabianism. The conclusion of this process of liquidationism was reached when between 1988 and 1991 they organisationally liquidated the Communist Party.

In 1981 the Leninists of the CPGB publicly announced their open, disciplined and principled struggle to reforge the Party. By its very nature a rebellion bound up with equipping the working class with a revolutionary programme. The CPGB we are seeking to build will organise the advanced part of the working class in Britain. It will not be a confessional sect. Nor will it be a pseudo-socialist extension of trade unionism. Informed by this understanding, the 4th Conference of the Leninists of the CPGB, meeting in December 1989, agreed to prepare a draft programme for the consideration of all workers, all left activists and all communists, which in due course would be presented to the refoundation congress of the CPGB.

Genuine communists never accepted the right of opportunists to deprive them of their Party membership nor their Party duties. The wrecking activity of the class collaborationists actually greatly increased the responsibilities of the revolutionary wing. Hence the 5th Conference of the Leninists of the CPGB, meeting in 1991, elected the Provisional Central Committee in order to revive Party work and rally new, healthy forces. A draft third programme was published in 1995. Subsequently, meeting in January 2011, the CPGB's Special Conference agreed this amended draft third programme - another milestone in the struggle to reforge the CPGB.

The CPGB's draft third programme is made up of six distinct but logically connected sections.

The first section outlines the main features of the epoch, the epoch of the transition from capitalism to communism. Then comes the nature of capitalism in Britain and the consequences of its development. Following on from here are the immediate political, social and economic measures required for winning the battle for democracy and ensuring that the market and the principle of capitalist profit is subordinated to the principle of human need. Such a minimum programme is, admittedly, technically feasible under capitalism. However, it can only be fully realised through the working class taking power, not only in Britain, but on a continental European scale.

From these radical foundations the character of the revolution and the position of the various classes and strata are presented. Next, again logically, comes the tasks of the CPGB in terms of the worldwide transition to communism. Here is the maximum programme. Finally the inescapable need for all partisans of the working class to unite in the Communist Party itself is dealt with. Our essential organisational principles are presented and show in no uncertain terms why the Communist Party is the most powerful weapon available to the working class.

All who accept this programme as a guide to action are urged to join us in this fight.

1 Our epoch

The present epoch is characterised by the revolutionary transition from capitalism to communism. The main contradiction is between a malfunctioning capitalism and an overdue communism.

Capitalism creates the abundant material wealth necessary for universal human freedom. Capitalism also creates its gravedigger, the working class. As imperialism, finance and monopoly capital superseded the period of mature capitalism in the late 19th century, it showed that the capitalist system was in decline and attempting to put off socialism by one means or the other.

The October 1917 revolution in Russia marked the beginning of the present epoch. Socialism was transformed from the realm of theory to that of practice. However, the workers' state in backward Russia was left in asphyxiating isolation. Social democracy betrayed the goal of socialism for the sake of gaining substantive reforms within capitalism. A whole raft of reforms were in fact conceded. The capitalist class was determined that there should be no more Octobers.

Meanwhile, imperialism sponsored civil war, armies of intervention and economic boycott to strangle socialism in its cradle. In besieged Russia, society could not find its way out of poverty towards abundance. Soviet society had to be militarised if it was to survive. Workers could not exercise democratic control over society. Indeed as a collectivity the working class decomposed. Under such conditions bureaucratic deformation was bound to occur. In the mid-20s, this isolation was theorised as 'socialism in one country', which became official policy in the Soviet Union. The symbolic link with the world revolution was broken. In the late 1920s Stalin oversaw a counterrevolution within the revolution. The re-enslaving of workers, the re-enserfing of peasants, monocracy, terror, the gulag and social madness followed.

Any lingering possibility of corrective reform closed. The eventual collapse of the Soviet Union in 1991 and the fate of similar regimes definitively confirms that there is no national road to communism.

1.1 Global economy

The world capitalist economy is an organic hierarchy based on exploitation and force. Depending on where they stand in the pecking order, countries play different roles in the imperialist system.

Though they remain viciously exploited, the under- and medium-developed countries now occupy a significant place in the world division of labour. And not only as suppliers of raw materials and agricultural products. Such countries now produce a wide range of manufactured goods. As a result the working class is now the majority class globally and has the self-interest to become a consciously international class.

A prerequisite for the final victory of the working class is winning power in the advanced countries. Only here has capitalism fully proletarianised the bulk of the population and accumulated the wealth needed for communism. The working class can come to power in backward or medium-developed countries. But such salients will prove short-lived unless revolution follows in advanced capitalist countries.

Capitalism develops through a series of booms and slumps. Government intervention reduces the depth and duration of slumps. However, simultaneously essential laws decline. Value, production for profit, private ownership and money are propped up by government intervention and bureaucratic organisation. The structural defects of capital lead the system to malfunction. The working class is faced with an historic choice: either take power and replace the market with the plan or suffer the ruinous consequences of capitalist decline and social disintegration.

1.2 Capitalist development

The world economy and capitalist development make the existence of countries and national borders increasingly anachronistic.

The continuous accumulation of capital means the social nature of production grows ever greater. Ownership and control is either taken into the hands of the state or becomes more and more international, institutionalised and concentrated.

Capitalist accumulation in no way implies the development of a rational system. Production is for the sake of production. Capital never rests, driven as it is by the unquenchable, vampire-like thirst for surplus value. It is a system of chronic overproduction that knows no intrinsic limits to exploitation. It is a system where dead labour turns against living labour, where money and profit are primary and need is incidental. It is a system of extreme alienation that dehumanises every human relationship.

Despite the abundance of its commodities and the wonders of modern technology, capitalism does not allow human beings to fulfil themselves as human beings. Work is often a dehumanising torture, not life's prime want. Although much hyped, leisure time is no more human.

Workers suffer relative pauperisation. Compared with capital, wages tend to shrink. As the world of things becomes ever greater, the world of people correspondingly becomes ever more insecure and atomised.

During periods of stagnation and crisis, through unemployment, wage cuts, intensification of labour, longer hours, temporary contracts, etc, capitalism assaults the existing cultural level of the masses - meagre and impoverished though it is. Hard-won wage rates, trade union rights and legal restrictions imposed on exploitation are damned as heresy by the high representatives of the dollar, euro, pound and yen. Hence capitalism threatens the workers even as a slave class.

Distorted by relations of exploitation and the lust for profit, national economies become not only anachronistic, but grossly lopsided. In the imperialist metropoles huge numbers are engaged in unproductive labour, such as banking, the stock market, insurance, advertising and marketing. In backward and medium-developed countries capitalism's destruction of peasant agriculture leaves hundreds of millions destitute and eking out a precarious existence in sprawling slums and shanty towns.

Thus capitalism advances the productive forces in a grossly inefficient, wasteful and inhuman way. The full development of humanity's powers requires the social control of production and planning, not only on a national, but an international scale.

1.3 The danger of war

War is the continuation of politics by other, violent, means. War is a sustained conflict on an extended scale. War is the product of class society. War, and the potential for war, will only end with the ending of class society itself.

Capitalism goes hand in hand with uneven development. Hence the constant pressure for a redivision of spoils. Rising 'have not' powers challenge the existing imperialist hierarchy and seek to offset their own problems at the expense of foreign rivals. When diplomacy and trade wars fail, military force decides. Trade blocs become military blocs. So imperialism means preparation for war. Peace is only a period of ceasefire. It is only the freezing of the division of spoils arrived at through war.

After 1945 imperialism normalised high levels of production of the means of destruction. Popular support for military Keynesianism was garnered through anti-communism and competition with the Soviet Union. The cold war became a system of social control east and west.

Capitalism now possesses weapons capable of destroying

human life across the whole planet. The struggle to end the danger of war by the working class is therefore a struggle for the survival of the human species.

Under communism the word 'war' will become redundant. So will the word 'peace'. The absence of war will gradually render obsolete its opposite, as humanity leaves behind its pre-history.

1.4 Nature

Nature is accorded no value by capital, which has but one interest - self-expansion. Capital has no intrinsic concern either for the worker or nature. Nature and the human being are nothing for capital except objects of exploitation.

Because of its never satisfied lust for profit capitalism results in the concentrated degradation of nature. Countless species of plants and animals have been driven to extinction. Many more are endangered. Deforestation, erosion of top soil, spread of deserts, overfishing of seas and oceans and anthropogenic air and water pollution have grown apace. In third-world cities that means deadly smogs, chronic bronchitis, emphysema and asthma. Huge numbers have no proper sanitation facilities and no ready access to clean drinking water.

Instead of cherishing the resources of nature there is plunder, waste, depletion and irresponsibility. Oil is criminally squandered through the car economy, huge areas of land are given over for growing biofuels, air travel booms, while public transport is typically neglected, and nuclear power is presented as the solution to global warming and the danger of runaway climate change.

Communists reject the claim that workers create all wealth under capitalism. There is also the wealth that comes from the labour of peasants, the petty bourgeoisie and middle class strata. Above that there is nature too.

Working class power presents the only viable alternative to the destructive reproduction of capital. To begin with as a countervailing force within capitalism that pulls against the logic of capital. The political economy of the working class brings with it not only higher wages and shorter hours. It brings health services, social security systems, pensions, universal primary and secondary education … and measures that protect the environment.

As well as being of capitalism, the working class is uniquely opposed to capitalism. The political economy of the working class more than challenges capital. It points beyond: to the total reorganisation of society and with that the ending of humanity's strained, brutalised and crisis-ridden relationship with nature.

1.5 The struggle against opportunism

Capitalism is objectively approaching communism. Yet achieving communism must be the conscious self-liberation of the working class. Communism needs the truth. Therefore the struggle against opportunism - that is, elevation of short-term or sectional interests over the general interest - is fundamental to the supersession of capitalism. The part must be subordinated to the whole, not the other way round. No country, no party, no trade union, no leader, no section of the working class takes precedence over the world revolution.

Because the communist revolution begins as a political act by an oppressed class its inevitability in no way implies that the negation of exploitation, alienation and unfreedom is mechanically assured.

Though, for example, the capitalist class is tiny, it possesses immense power - and not only in the form of wealth and the state machine. As the ruling class, its ideas are the ruling ideas. Capitalist ideas are spontaneously generated and in the battle for hearts and minds are carefully cultivated by a paid army of permanent persuaders - the media, education, the arts, religion, establishment parties, etc.

In contrast, numerically the working class is a giant. It can, like any slave class, economically and politically fight to better its conditions within the existing system. Yet to realise itself as a class for itself, a class with an historic mission to free humanity, it must acquire a scientific, a rational, a rounded world outlook. That cannot be gained except through an open struggle against wrong ideas. This must encompass the struggle against manifestations of opportunism within our own, national and international, communist ranks.

1.6 World revolution

World revolution is the fight to liberate humanity. It is a process whereby capitalism is replaced by communism.

The victory of socialist revolution in one or more country is only partial until the balance of forces has tilted decisively against capitalism. That means the socialist revolution must triumph in a tranche of advanced countries if it is not to suffer deformation and counterrevolution in one form or another. National revolutions are therefore best coordinated and where possible synchronised.

2 Capitalism in Britain

Due to a combination of social, political, economic and other factors, Britain was the first country to be dominated by a real, fully mature, capitalism.

By the first half of the 19th century the mass of the population had already been expropriated from the land. Denied any possibility of an independent existence, to survive, they had to sell the only commodity they possessed - the ability to work. Herded into factories, mines and mills, they were subjected to ruthless exploitation. Aristocratic and mercantile wealth gained from piracy, colonial plunder and the trade in black slaves became capital used to suck the life energy from wage workers. Vast fortunes were amassed.

British capital was able to secure a hitherto unprecedented position in the world market. Britain truly was the workshop of the world. Inevitably, Britain was chased by rivals - most notably Germany and the United States. Britain was no longer the undisputed world hegemon. Still the most powerful capitalist state, but visibly suffering relative decline.

Increasingly Britain experienced difficulties in accumulating capital. To overcome that and delay working class revolution the ruling classes turned to the restriction of competition and a greatly expanded overseas empire. As part of this the export of commodities was eclipsed in importance by the export of capital itself. Finance capital came to dominance.

Britain carved out a gigantic empire that at its peak

covered one-quarter of the earth's land surface and included one-quarter of its population. There was additionally an unofficial empire of subordinate and dependent countries.

The empire was a source of cheap raw materials and army recruits. It was also a safe market that could be administratively closed to rivals. It spawned an overblown bureaucratic-military superstructure, staffed by the aristocratic products of Britain's public schools. Furthermore the super-, or extra profits gained from robbing the colonies and returns from the export of capital provided the wherewithal needed to ameliorate class antagonisms at home.

Inexorably Britain's rivals began to experience similar problems and seek out their own expansionist solutions. By the dawn of the 20th century the world was effectively divided. Inter-imperialist contradictions came to a bloody climax. In two devastating world wars tens of millions were butchered in the interests of capital. Barbarism took on capitalist form.

Britain saw off two challenges from Germany in 1914-18 and 1939-45. Despite that Britain lost out to the US. After Europe had exhausted itself, so strong was US imperialism that it had no need for a formal empire and could relatively peacefully go about the redivision of the whole capitalist world. The conditions for the post-World War II long boom were laid.

2.1 Social and political consequences of Britain's imperialist development

From the second half of the 19th century onwards Britain's industrial monopoly and then its empire enabled the governing elite to tame the spontaneous working class movement. Being able to bribe directly and indirectly a wide section of the working class, it could keep expectations within the parameters of the existing system. The revolutionary tradition of Chartism gave way to the reformist tradition of narrow trade unionism. Consolidation of a trade union bureaucracy - merchants in wage labour - only served to reinforce retrogression.

The revolutionary, communist, militant trend on occasion

posed a threat to the stability of capitalism. Despite that, throughout the 20th century Labourism and the Labour Party dominated the workers' movement. Labourism has often deployed socialistic rhetoric. It is, however, a thoroughly reactionary, pro-capitalist ideology. In war and peace, in government and opposition, the Labour leadership has loyally served the interests of British imperialism. What reform legislation it introduced was designed to dampen, not fire, the class struggle.

Britain managed decolonisation in the midst of an unprecedented boom. There was no crisis of empire. It was moreover able to achieve high rates of economic growth and put in place a social democratic settlement. In a negative and perverted way capitalism anticipated and carried out some of the measures of socialism - cheap housing allocated according to a points system, healthcare based on need, free comprehensive education, an ethos of equality, etc.

Because it was closely aligned to the new US hegemon, British capitalism was able to maintain its parasitic relationship with the rest of the world. Banking, insurance and the stock market were of far greater size and importance in Britain than in comparable countries. Integration into Europe was, however, undertaken from a position of weakness, not strength. Britain could not dominate Europe economically or politically. But it could act as a US Trojan horse to prevent deeper European unity.

When the post-World War II boom came to an end, Britain no longer enjoyed the option it had in the 1930s of cushioning itself through the system of empire preference. British capitalism had to renew the class struggle at home. A whole swathe of Britain's industrial base was sacrificed so as to undermine trade union power.

To enforce the rollback of the social democratic settlement all manner of authoritarian measures were enacted - laws against trade union activity, laws limiting free speech, laws curbing demonstrations. Reversal of the social democratic settlement proves yet again that reforms workers gain under capitalism are liable to be lost, given new conditions.

3 Immediate demands

Capitalism creates the necessity amongst workers to engage in constant struggle. Even without communist leadership class battles will occur, albeit at an elemental level.

However, to liberate themselves workers must fight for the positive resolution of all social contradictions, first and foremost by winning the battle for democracy.

3.1 Democracy

Under capitalism democracy exhibits two sides. There is mystification, whereby the masses are reconciled to their exploitation and fooled into imagining themselves to be the sovereign power in society. On the other hand, there is the struggle to give democratic forms a new, substantive, content. This can only be achieved by the working class taking the lead in the fight to ensure popular control over all aspects of society.

Hence, communists do not counterpose democracy to socialism. Democracy is much more than voting every four or five years. Democracy is the rule of the people, for the people, by the people. To make that aspiration real necessarily means removing all judicial, structural and socio-economic restraints on, or distortions of, popular control from below.

3.1.1 Winning the battle for democracy

Communists stand for republican democracy. That means demanding:

- Abolition of the monarchy and the House of Lords, and a single-chamber parliament with proportional representation, annual elections and MPs' salaries set at the level of a skilled worker.
- No to the presidential prime minister. End prime ministerial appointment of ministers and all other forms of prime ministerial patronage.
- Disband MI5, MI6, special branch and the entire secret state apparatus.
- For local democracy. Service provision, planning, tax raising, law enforcement and funding allocation to be radically devolved downwards as far as possible and appropriate: to ward, borough, city and county levels.

3.1.2 Freedom
The interests of the working class require the open struggle of ideas and the ability to freely organise.

Therefore communists demand:
- Unrestricted freedom of speech, publication, conscience, association and assembly.
- An end to state bans and censorship. No laws against 'hate speech', which will inevitably be turned against the workers movement and the left.
- No bans on controversial organisations and individuals in civil society institutions such as universities and student unions. Bigoted and reactionary viewpoints must be fought in the open, not via bureaucratic no-platform, safeguarding or safe spaces policies.
- Oppose state secrets. Demand free access to all state files, cabinet papers, diplomatic agreements, etc.
- Abolish copyright laws, patents and other so-called intellectual property rights.
- Socialisation of internet service providers, public cloud infrastructure and other natural monopolies in communications. An end to the corruption of advertising-funded media.

3.1.3 The national question

As a general rule communists do not want to see countries broken up into small nation-states. Ours is the revolutionary call for humanity to shed the flag-waving, imagined community of the nation-state.

Communists are the most consistent internationalists and unreservedly denounce any tactical pandering to, let alone attempts to exacerbate, national tensions.

Communists want a positive solution to the national question in the interests of the working class: that is, the merging of nations. That can only be achieved through democracy and the right of all to fully develop their own culture.

Where national questions exist, communists fight to secure the right of nations to self-determination. Historically constituted peoples should be able to freely decide their own destiny. They can separate if they so wish. Thereby they can also elect to come together or stay together with others.

3.1.4 England, Scotland and Wales

The British nation evolved from the gradual bonding of the English, Welsh and Scottish. Drawn together over centuries by common political and economic experience, they now in the main possess a common language, culture and psychology.

The birth of the British nation was a progressive development objectively. Nevertheless, because it was carried out under the aegis of a brutal absolutism it was accompanied by countless acts of violence and discrimination.

As post-boom British imperialism was forced to turn inwards, and in the absence of a viable proletarian alternative, resistance in Scotland and Wales often took a national form. A mythologised past was deployed by nationalists, opportunists and Labourites alike to serve their nefarious purposes.

Communists stand opposed to every form of Scottish and Welsh national narrow-mindedness. Equally we oppose every form of British/English national chauvinism. Ideas of exclusiveness or superiority, national oppression itself, obscure the fundamental antagonism between labour and capital, and divert attention from the need to unite against the common enemy - the British capitalist state.

While communists defend the right of Scotland and Wales to secede, we do not want separation. Communists want the closest union circumstances allow. The peoples of Scotland and Wales cannot decide their future democratically through the monarchy and the Westminster parliament of the House of Commons and House of Lords. That is why we stand for a federal republic of England, Scotland and Wales.

It is the proletarian-internationalist duty of communists in Scotland and Wales to defend the right of the Scots and Welsh to remain with and achieve an even higher degree of unity with the English. Correspondingly communists in England must be the best defenders of the right of Scotland and Wales to separate. That in no way contradicts the duty to advocate unity.

3.1.5 Ireland
Ireland is Britain's oldest colony. In 1921 Ireland was dissected - a sectarian Six County statelet was created in order to permanently divide the Irish working class and perpetuate British domination over the whole island of Ireland.

We communists in Britain unconditionally support the right of the people of Ireland to reunite. Working class opposition to British imperialism in Ireland is a necessary condition for our own liberation - a nation that oppresses another can never itself be free. The struggle for socialism in Britain and national liberation in Ireland are closely linked.

Communists in Ireland likewise have internationalist duties. They must fight for the friendship between workers in Britain and Ireland and their speediest coming together. They must be resolute opponents of nationalism.

3.1.6 Europe
Far from pushing through the unity of Europe capitalism has held back what is objectively necessary. National rivalries,

short-term interests, stoking-up national chauvinism and subordination to US imperialism has allowed for nothing more than a weak, creaking, bickering quasi-democratic European Union.

Communists stand for the abolition of the EU commission and council of ministers, of the treaties which require unanimous agreement of states to amend them, and of the unaccountable Court of Justice. Instead we seek a united Europe democratically ruled by the working class.

Towards that end we have a vital interest in organising across Europe: trade unions; cooperatives; campaigns for the levelling up of wages, conditions and rights; coordination between communist groups and parties; etc.

No European country alone is capable of taking decisive action on a global scale. Those days are long gone and will never return. True, a workers' Europe might be subject to blockades and attempts to isolate it, but that will not be easy. The flame of liberation will surely spread to Asia, Africa and the Americas.

3.2 Peace

British imperialism has an unparalleled history of war and aggression in virtually every corner of the world. Though no longer the power it once was, large, well equipped armed forces are maintained in order to serve the interests of British capitalism abroad and at home.

British capitalism is one of the world's main weapons manufacturers and exporters. It has a vested interest in promoting militarism. Communists stress, however, that the struggle against the military-industrial complex cannot be separated from the struggle against the profit system as a whole.

Communists oppose all imperialist wars, military alliances and occupations. We also reject nuclear, biological and other such weapons of mass destruction as inherently inhuman.

Peace cannot come courtesy of bodies such as the United Nations - an assembly of exploiters and murderers. It is the duty of communists to connect the popular desire for peace with the aim of revolution. Only by disarming the bourgeoisie and through the victory of international socialism can the danger of war be eliminated.

Communists are not pacifists. Everywhere we support just wars, above all revolutionary civil wars for socialism. Communists will therefore strive to expose the war preparations of the bourgeoisie, the lies of social imperialists and illusions fostered by social pacifism.

3.3 Environmental crisis

Global warming and the danger of runaway climate change have to be dealt with as a matter of extreme urgency. But we should be on guard against pseudo-solutions. Carbon offsets and carbon trading amount to greenwashing capitalism. Blaming population numbers in poor countries easily leads to Malthusian programmes and terrible human suffering. Launching reflective aerosols into the stratosphere, ocean mirrors, cloud thinning and space sunshades would, quite probably, lead to unintended, potentially irreversible, consequences.

Instead communists present these demands:

● Rapidly transition away from coal, oil, gas and nuclear power towards wind, tidal, solar, geothermal and other renewables.

● Reduce energy demand: bring home and work closer together, support workers who want flexible working arrangements; encourage online meetings, cycling, walking and staycations; introduce free local and urban public transport; discourage the consumption of meat and dairy products; put limits on air travel and car use; ensure that the existing housing stock is radically upgraded and exacting building standards are enforced; impose swingeing taxes on big scale polluters.

● Aim to go beyond carbon neutral as soon as possible.

● Where feasible, rewild: forests, natural floodplains, marshes, fens and heath land should be re-established. Strive to reintroduce the full array of native flora and fauna. Grouse moors, deer-stalking estates and upland sheep runs would be prime targets for returning to nature.

• Concrete jungles, urban sprawl, using rivers and seas as common sewers, huge farms and intensive meat and dairy production result in substantial damage to the biosphere. Nationalise the land and waterways.

• Towns and cities should be full of trees, roof gardens, planted walls, allotments, wild parks and small-scale cooperative farms.

• Destructive fishing practices such as bottom trawling should be banned. Inshore seas must include wide no-catch areas. The aim should be to fully restore marine life and thus create a sustainable fishing industry.

3.4 Working conditions and wage workers

Communists begin with what workers need, not what capitalism can afford.

Therefore communists demand:

• A maximum five-day working week and a maximum seven-hour day for all wage workers. Reduction of that to a four-day working week and a maximum six-hour day for occupations which are dangerous or particularly demanding. The working day must include rest periods of not less than two hours.

• An uninterrupted weekly break of not less than 65 hours for all wage workers.

• Equal pay for equal work.

• Abolition of overtime in its present form. In the case of emergencies and other such eventualities overtime must be voluntary, for only short periods and with at least double pay.

• A minimum net wage to be set on the basis of what is needed by a worker and one child to lead a full life, participating materially and culturally in society. All benefits, pensions and student grants to at least match the minimum wage.

• A minimum of six weeks' fully paid holiday leave during the year in addition to public holidays.

• Insurance and other such payments to be made entirely by

the capitalists and the state.
- Occupational training for all workers to be a legal obligation for employers.
- Child labour to be illegal. For young people aged between 14 and 16, the working week should be limited to five days and the working day to no more than two hours.
- All industrial courts, arbitration panels, etc to be made up of at least 50% elected workers' representatives.
- All workers must have the right to strike and to join a trade union.

3.5 Migrant workers and racism

Large numbers of workers who have come from other countries live in Britain. Migration is often the result of poverty, lack of opportunity, war or persecution.

Capital moves around the world without restriction. As a matter of principle communists are for the free movement of people and against all measures preventing them entering or leaving countries. Simultaneously, we seek to end poverty, lack of opportunity, war and persecution everywhere.

The bourgeoisie uses migrant workers, especially illegals, as worst paid labour. That is ensured through immigration laws and quotas, lack of security and police raids, detention centres and deportations.

The capitalist state in Britain now has an official ideology of anti-racism. Of course, racism still exists, as does the national chauvinist consensus which champions British imperialism's interests against foreign rivals and sets worker against worker.

Migrant workers are not the problem. The capitalists who use them to increase competition between workers are. The reformist plea for non-racist immigration controls plays directly into the hands of our exploiters. It concedes the right of the state to bar workers from entering Britain.

It is in the interest of all workers that migrant workers and ethnic communities are integrated. Assimilation is progressive as long as it is not based upon force. In order to encourage integration and strengthen the unity of the

working class, the following demands are put forward:
● The right to speak and be educated in one's own language. The right to conduct correspondence with the state in one's own language.
● The right to learn English for all migrant workers and their families. Employers must provide language courses.
● The right to become citizens with full social and political rights for all workers who have resided in the country for six months.
● Fight all discrimination based on race, ethnicity or culture by state or private bodies.

3.6 The unemployed

Unemployment is an integral feature of capitalism. In periods of crisis millions cannot be profitably employed and are discarded. At all times unemployment is capitalism's principal tool for collectively disciplining the working class and maximising exploitation. Full employment, whether as a result of deliberate government policy - as in the post-war period - or in periods of exceptional economic boom, increases the confidence of workers and the strength of their organisations, leading to higher wages and improved conditions.

Permanent full employment is not compatible with the continuation of capitalism. The capitalist class and its state will therefore act to restore the reserve army of labour to counter the combativeness of the organised working class.

Maintained at below subsistence levels, the unemployed increasingly constitute a permanently marginalised section of the population. The only way to eradicate unemployment is to end the system that causes and requires it.

As part of the working class the unemployed must be integrated as fully as possible into the workers' movement.

They must be made into a reserve army of the revolution by demanding:
● The right to work at trade union rates of pay or unemployment benefit at the level of the minimum wage.
● No state harassment of the unemployed. Claiming benefit

is a right, not a privilege.
- Cheap labour schemes must be replaced by real training and education under trade union supervision.
- The unemployed must have the right to remain in or join trade unions as full members with equal rights.
- To the extent that they operate, unemployed workers' organisations must be represented in the trade union movement - from trades councils to the Trade Union Congress.

3.7 Nationalisation

The historic task of the working class is to fully socialise the giant transnational corporations, and programmes for wholesale nationalisation can only succeed in breaking such corporations into inefficient national units. From the point of view of world revolution, programmes for wholesale nationalisation are today objectively reactionary. Our starting point is the most advanced achievements of capitalism. Globalised production needs global social control.

Communists oppose the illusion that nationalisation equates in some way with socialism. There is nothing inherently progressive or socialistic about nationalised industries.

However, specific acts of nationalisation can serve the interests of workers. We call for the nationalisation of the land, banks and financial services, along with basic infrastructure, such as public transport, electricity, gas and water supplies.

Faced with plans for closure, mass sackings and threats of capital flight communists demand:
- No redundancies. Nationalise threatened workplaces or industries under workers' control.
- Compensation to former owners should be paid only in cases of proven need.
- There must be no business secrets hidden from the workers. Open the books and data banks to the inspection of specialists appointed by and responsible to the workers.

3.8 Housing

Communists regard the provision of housing as a basic right.

Towards this end we demand:

● A massive revival of council and other social house building programmes. The shortage of housing must be ended.

● Council and social housing must be high quality, energy-efficient and with spacious rooms. Where appropriate, outside areas must be provided for children to play.

● Accommodation to be allocated on the basis of need and rents set at a token level. There should be life-long tenure.

● Communal housing schemes with shared services, gardens, swimming pools, gyms, etc should be included as part of the mix of housing options.

● Housing estates and blocks of flats should be democratically run by tenants in conjunction with the local authorities and relevant trade unions.

● Architects should be encouraged to innovate and use their imagination. However, the design of all new builds and the refurbishment of existing accommodation should fully involve future residents and the wider local community.

● A publicly-owned building corporation to be established to ensure that planned targets for house-building are reached and to provide permanent employment and ongoing training for building workers.

3.9 Health

Communists demand a comprehensive, free and democratic health service to meets the needs of everyone.

Communists therefore present the following demands:

● The national health service must provide the highest quality care in all areas, including dentistry, optometry and those complementary therapies that have been scientifically proven to be effective.

● The NHS must place a strong emphasis on preventative interventions.

● All NHS hospitals to be run by their staff and the community they serve.

- For NHS community clinics providing a full range of health services democratically accountable to local people.
- GPs, hospital doctors, consultants, etc who work in the NHS should be exclusively employed by the NHS.
- The pharmaceutical industry should be nationalised, so that the development of drugs serves human need, not the generation of profits.

3.10 Trade unions

Trade unions limit competition between workers, thus securing a better price for labour-power. They represent a tremendous gain for the working class, drawing millions of workers into collective activity against employers.

Of course, left to itself, trade union consciousness is characterised by sectionalism. At best trade union consciousness attempts to constantly improve the lot of workers within capitalism. At worst trade union consciousness degenerates into business unionism and sacrificing the interests of workers for the sake of capitalist competitiveness and profitability.

Communists openly seek to make trade unions into schools for communism. They do this by always putting forward the general interest, by fighting for workers' unity and by fully involving the rank and file in decision-making.

Bargaining is a specialist activity. Consequently the trade unions need a layer of functionaries. However, due to lack of democratic control and accountability these functionaries have consolidated themselves into a conservative caste.

The trade union bureaucracy is more concerned with amicable deals and preserving union funds than with the class struggle. Operating as an intermediary between labour and capital, it has a real, material interest in the continued existence of the wage system.

Within the trade unions communists fight against bureaucracy by demanding:
- Trade unions must be free of any interference or control by the state or employer.
- No trade union official to be paid above the average wage

of a worker in that particular union.
- All full-time trade union officials must be elected, accountable and instantly recallable.
- Workers should support trade union leaders only to the extent that they fight for the long-term interests of the working class as a whole.
- All-embracing workplace committees. Organise all workers, whatever their trade, whether or not they are in trade unions. Workplace committees should fight to exercise control over hiring and firing, production and investment.
- One industry, one union. Industrial unions are rational and enhance the ability of workers to struggle.
- Given the international nature of the capitalist system and the existence of giant transnational companies, trade unions also need to organise internationally.

3.11 Councils of action

In any decisive clash of class against class, new forms of organisation which are higher, more general, more flexible than trade unions emerge. In Russia they have been called soviets, in Germany Räte, in Britain councils of action.

Embracing and coordinating all who are in struggle, such organisations have the potential to become institutions in the future workers' state. Communists encourage any such development.

3.12 Militia

Communists are against the standing army and for the armed people. This principle will never be realised voluntarily by the capitalist state. It has to be won, in the first place by the working class developing its own militia.

Such a body grows out of the class struggle itself: defending picket lines, mass demonstrations, workplace occupations, fending off fascists, etc.

As the class struggle intensifies, conditions are created for the workers to arm themselves and win over sections of the military forces of the capitalist state. Every opportunity must be used to take even tentative steps towards this goal. As circumstances allow, the working class must equip itself with all weaponry necessary to bring about revolution.

To facilitate this we demand:

● Rank and file personnel in the state's armed bodies must be protected from bullying, humiliating treatment and being used against the working class.

● There must be full trade union and democratic rights, including the right to form bodies such as soldiers' councils.

● The privileges of the officer caste must be abolished. Officers must be elected. Workers in uniform must become the allies of the masses in struggle.

● The people have the right to bear arms and defend themselves.

● The dissolution of the standing army and the formation of a popular militia under democratic control.

3.13 Women

Women are oppressed because of the system of exploitation and the division of labour. Women's oppression has existed since the dawn of class society. Ending exploitation will mark the beginning of women's emancipation. Therefore the struggle for both is interconnected.

Women's emancipation is not a question for women alone. Just as the abolition of class exploitation is of concern to female workers, so the emancipation of women is of concern to male workers. The struggle for socialism and the emancipation of women cannot be separated.

Women carry the main burden of feeding babies, house management, supermarket buying, family cooking, child ferrying, etc, which is performed gratis. Such work is often frantic, demoralising and allows no kind of rounded, cultural development.

Advanced capitalism has created the material prerequisites for the liberation of women. However, women cannot be fully emancipated until the disappearance of the division of labour and without going beyond bourgeois right, which entails: 'To each according to work done'.

In Britain women have won or been granted formal equality with men. But the capitalist system often makes a mockery of that. At work, at home, in trade unions, in official politics, in culture, in organised religion, women still find themselves disadvantaged, facing bias and inequality.

There has been a rapid increase in women's participation in the economy. As a norm therefore women are exploited by capital as cheap wage workers and domestic slaves. Hence they suffer a double burden.

Women, therefore, have their own problems and demands. These demands do not conflict with the demands of the working class: rather they reinforce them.

Communists say:

● Turn formal equality into genuine equality. Socially, economically, politically and culturally there must be substantive equality.

● Open free, 24-hour crèches and kindergartens to facilitate full participation in social life outside the home. Open high-quality canteens with cheap prices. Establish laundry and house-cleaning services undertaken by local authorities and the state. This to be the first step in the socialisation of housework. We would encourage a balance of male and female workers to be employed in these facilities.

● Fully paid maternity leave of 12 months, which the mother can choose to take from up to three months before giving birth. The partner to be provided with six months fully paid paternity leave - three months of which should be compulsory - to encourage equality and bonding with the child.

● Free abortion and contraception on demand.

● Provision for either parent, or main carer, to be allowed paid leave to look after sick children.

● A maximum six-hour working day for all nursing mothers.

● Full support for women fleeing violence within the home.

33

3.14 Youth and education

Youth are used as cheap labour, sexually policed and blamed for social decay. The system also exploits youth as consumers. Every ideal, every artistic talent is judged in terms of generating artificial needs. There are many who reject the twisted values of the system. But in despair this often turns to nihilism and escapism - themselves turned into commodities by capitalism.

Youth are at the sharp end of capitalist decline. Young workers are in general less likely to be protected by trade union membership. Homelessness, unemployment and sexual abuse are greatly disproportionate amongst the young.

The education system is a vitally important site of struggle. Secondary education is narrow, unimaginative and obsessively focused on targets and exams. Official schemes for unemployed youth are notoriously mediocre, designed more to massage government statistics than equip young workers with the skills they need for a worthwhile future.

Higher education is increasingly designed to suit the commercial interests of employers - university courses included. This sector churns out the next generation of skilled workers. Elite universities specialise in the reproduction of the upper-middle and ruling classes. Not surprisingly, here something like a proper education is on offer.

The following demands are of crucial importance for youth:

● Compulsory education up until the age of 16 and from then on within a fully democratic system. Secondary education should be of a polytechnical nature. That is, rounded to include technical and personal skills, as well as scientific, social, historical and artistic subjects. Tertiary education should be a right, not a privilege. Abolish student fees. Everyone should be encouraged to develop themselves and their intellectual and critical abilities to the fullest degree.

● For academic freedom in teaching and research.

● Students over the age of 16 should receive grants set at the level of the minimum wage.

● No state funding, charitable status or tax breaks for religious and private schools and colleges.

- Provision of housing/hostels for youth to enter of their own choice for longer or shorter periods when they lose their parents or choose to leave them.
- The right of every young person on leaving education to a job, proper technical training or full benefits.
- Remove all obstacles to the participation of youth in social life. Votes and the right to be elected from the age of 16.
- The provision of a broad range of sports and cultural centres under the control of representatives elected by youth.
- Young people are entitled to develop their sexual lives free from parental, police or religious control. We favour legislation which protects children and young people from sexual exploitation by those who are substantially older than them, especially by those in authority over them.
- We defend contraception services which are free and confidential. We fight for extensive provision of education, counselling and advice on all matters relating to sexuality and reproduction.

3.15 Pensioners and the elderly

People deserve a secure, dignified and comfortable old age. The needs of the elderly should be met fully by the state and be available by right. Old people must not suffer the humiliation and anxiety of relying on means tests or charity.

The aim of these demands is to mobilise the working class as a whole to fight for pensioners' rights:
- No compulsory retirement on the basis of age. Right to retirement from age 60 for all workers - at 55 in unpleasant and dangerous occupations.
- The state pension should be set at the level of the minimum wage, and should be paid to everyone who has reached retirement age and wants to give up work.
- Old people should have the right to decide how they live. The state must provide what is needed to allow elderly people to live independently if they so wish, for as long as they are physically or mentally capable of doing so. There should be no compulsory institutionalisation.
- Social clubs for the elderly should be democratic and

subsidised by the state, not charities.
● The comfort and dignity of the dying must be ensured at all times. Euthanasia and disposal of the body after death should be carried out according to the wishes of the individual.

3.16 Sexual freedom

Gay men, lesbians, bisexuals, transgender people, etc have often been scapegoated or persecuted. They are portrayed as threats to timeless religious values, sexual norms and the nuclear family - the basic economic unit of capitalist society.

Bigoted attitudes divide the working class and aid those advocating the authoritarian state. The working class needs to be mobilised in order to defend and advance sexual freedom.

Communists demand:
● Decriminalisation of all consensual sexual practices. End police and state harassment.
● Lesbian women and gay men should be accorded the same rights in society as heterosexuals: that is, state marriages, artificial insemination for lesbians, adoption and fostering. No discrimination in custody cases on the grounds of sexual orientation.
● No discrimination in any area of employment.
● Decriminalisation of prostitution so as to remove it from criminal control. For the self-organisation of prostitutes to improve their conditions. Prostitutes to be provided with special healthcare and other services to reduce the dangers they confront. Measures must be put in place to give prostitutes wider social opportunities.

3.17 Crime and prison

Crime can only be understood in relationship to society. In class society crime is a product of alienation, want or resistance. Under capitalism the criminal justice system is anti-working class, irrational and inhuman. Property is considered primary; the person merely a form of property.

Against this communists demand:
- The codification of criminal law. Judges cannot be allowed to 'rediscover' old offences or invent new ones.
- All judges and magistrates must be subject to election and recall.
- Defend and extend the jury system. Anyone charged with an offence that carries the possibility of a prison sentence can elect for a jury trial.
- Fines to be proportionate to income.
- Too many people are unnecessarily in prison. A high proportion of prisoners lack basic literacy skills, have mental health issues or suffer from an alcohol or drug problem.
- Prison should always be considered a last resort.
- End the war on drugs. Recreational drugs should be legalised and quality standards assured. People with a dependency problem should be offered treatment not given a criminal record.
- There must be workers' supervision of prisons. Prisoners must be allowed the maximum opportunity to develop themselves as human beings. People should only be imprisoned within a short distance of their home locality - if not, families must be given full cost of travel for visits.
- Prison life must be made as near normal as possible. The aim of prison should be rehabilitation, not punishment.
- Prisoners should have the right to vote in parliamentary and other such elections and to stand for election. Votes from prisoners to count within the constituency where they actually live, not where they happen to originate.

3.18 Religion

Unlike previous oppressed classes in history religion can play no progressive role for the working class in its struggle against today's ruling class.

Nevertheless, though communists want to overcome all religious prejudices, we are the most consistent defenders of the individual's freedom of conscience and freedom of worship.

Communists therefore demand:

● The establishment of a secular state - ie, the separation of church and state. Confiscate all Church of England property not directly related to acts of worship: eg, land holdings, share portfolios and art treasures. End all state subsidies for religious institutions.

● Freedom for all religious cults. Freedom for atheistic propaganda. Religious organisations and individuals have the right to propagate their ideas and seek to win converts. Opponents of religion have the same right.

● End all state-sponsored religious propaganda and acts of worship. Religion is a private, not a state matter. Religion can be studied as a subject of academic interest in state schools, not as a means to indoctrinate children.

3.19 Small businesses and farms

Small business people, including small farmers, form a petty bourgeois stratum in Britain. Carrying on an unstable, precarious existence, these people operate in subordination to monopoly capital.

The petty bourgeoisie works alone, alongside family members or with a few hired employees. A combination of the threat of bankruptcy and an aspiration to become big capitalists drives them to work and work: often longer hours and in worse conditions than many members of the working class.

Every downward oscillation of the capitalist economy confronts the petty bourgeoisie with financial ruin. While the destruction of this stratum is economically progressive, the working class has a political interest to defend the petty bourgeoisie from the abuses and manipulations of big capital and the banks, at the same time fighting to improve the working conditions, security of employment and living standards of wage workers in farming and small businesses.

Communists demand:

● Secure rights of tenure for owner-occupiers, small farmers and small businesses, with low rents.

● Cancellation of debts to banks arising from disproportionately high interest rates. Provision of low interest rates for small businesses.

● Guaranteed prompt payment of bills by big business to small businesses.

● Encouragement for the formation of producers' cooperatives through the provision of scientific and technical advice, research facilities, administrative machinery, grants for capital improvements, etc.

4 Character of the Revolution

There are no get-rich-quick solutions to establish working class rule and, eventually, communism. Coups or takeover attempts by a minority are bound to fail, as is participation in capitalist coalition governments.

Capitalism can only be superseded by the working class uniting itself internationally and rallying all who are oppressed. Without working class rule there can be no socialism, no human freedom, no ecologically sustainable production, no end to exploitation.

Only a revolution supported by the large majority can establish socialism. We fully support the battle cry of the Chartists: 'Peacefully if we can, forcefully if we must.'

4.1 Classes in the revolution

The working class is the only consistently revolutionary section of society. Without owning any of the means of production of society, it has nothing to lose but its chains. Of course, left to itself, left to spontaneity, it is riven with sectionalism and exists merely as a slave class, capable of being economically militant, even insurrectionary, but not hegemonic. What makes it a hegemonic class is unity around the communist programme.

The working class constitutes a large majority of the population in Britain - as well as in Europe, the US, Japan and other advanced capitalist powers. The working class consists of not only the employed, but the non-employed

- pensioners, those on sickness and unemployment benefit, carers looking after young children or aged relatives, students being trained for the labour market, etc.

Traditional distinctions between manual and non-manual work are more and more irrelevant because of social development. Hence besides manual industrial workers the working class also includes workers in the health service, transport, the civil service and local government, as well as non-manual workers in industry, finance and distribution, such as technicians, clerical and sales staff.

If the working class does not elevate itself from being a slave class, it finds its common actions paralysed or limited by opposing competitive interests, which divide every section against every other section.

The capitalist class - those who live by exploiting labour power and who serve the self-expansion of capital - are very small in number. But history, wealth, positions of corporate power, connections with the state make it the ruling class, and the class whose ideas rule society.

There are, however, deep internal contradictions. Not only is capitalist pitted against capitalist in the market, but finance capital exploits industrial capital and big capital exploits medium and small capital.

What does this mean for small and medium capitalists?

On the one hand, medium and small capitalists suffer due to their disadvantageous position in the market and lack of an intimate relationship with the state. On the other, they benefit from big capital's global reach and ability to pacify the working class.

All capitalists are united in needing the working class to remain wage slaves in perpetuity. So, as well as contradictions, there are common interests. Contradictions are secondary.

This is mirrored politically. Medium and small capitalists are united behind the monopolies and great financial corporations. They have no real independent voice. Ideologically narrow-minded, the small capitalists try to influence society through institutions which are in the main entirely subordinate to big capital.

The task of communists is to break the working class from the influence of all sections of the bourgeoisie. There can be no strategic alliance with the medium and small capitalists. Individuals from the bourgeoisie can come over to the side of the working class, but never any section of it. However, the working class can and should take advantage of the contradictions within the bourgeoisie. Some capitalists may support giving in to demands of the working class, though this damages other capitalists. Concessions open up fissures in the ranks of our enemy and help to neutralise sections of it.

The middle class, including the classic petty bourgeoisie - the self-employed, lawyers and other professionals, career criminals - and also middle management, middle-grade civil servants, trade union officials - shades into the bourgeoisie at its upper end and into the working class at the lower. Inevitably it wavers between the two main classes in society. To the extent that it has its own political programme, it is based on reactionary and utopian calls for a return to small, family production and national independence.

As capitalism relentlessly revolutionises the circumstances of production, elements within the middle class find old, privileged positions being dissolved. Such a process gives rise to explosive shifts and political intervention can speed the process of proletarianisation. Economic crises plunge the middle class into turmoil and into political action.

Workers ought to seek, as opportunities present themselves, alliances with the various organisations and manifestations of these intermediate strata. Indeed the working class must represent the middle class against capital in so far as this does not contradict its own interests.

The middle class can under no circumstances be regarded a consistent ally of the working class. That said, success in prising it away from capital deprives our main enemy of a major social prop and adds to the momentum of revolution.

4.2 The working class constitution

This section outlines the form of organisation of the state and political life. It represents the culmination and continuation of our immediate demands.

Incongruous as it might seem, the aim of this constitution is to facilitate its own negation. The constitution of the workers' state will become simply a piece of paper, an historical document, as the state withers away along with classes.

The principles of our constitution are not gleaming abstractions nor a utopian dream. They are born out of a scientific understanding of the class struggle and reflect real historic experience. Crucially that the seizure of state power is not the final culmination of the class struggle.

Communists fight to achieve the following:

● Supreme power in the state will be a single popular assembly composed of delegates who are elected and recallable at any time. Pay of delegates will be no greater than the average skilled worker.

● All parties which accept the laws of the new revolutionary order as binding will be free to operate. We accept the possibility of one party or coalition of parties replacing another peacefully. Minorities have the right and should be given the opportunity to become majorities.

● There must be no financial penalties to inhibit standing in elections. There should be an open count.

● Local organs of government must have a wide degree of autonomy.

● The principle of openness in state affairs will be guaranteed.

● All international agreements counter to the interests of the working class will be abrogated.

● There will be no censorship. There must be the right to communicate on all topics.

● The existing armed forces and the police will be disbanded. In their place there will be a people's militia that will embody the right of everyone to bear arms.

4.3 Economic measures

The workers' state inherits not only sectors of the economy that capitalism has socialised in its own way, but those sectors owned by small and medium capital and the petty bourgeoisie as well as a middle class which possesses various skills monopolies. Under these conditions universal nationalisation, forced collectivisation and flat-wage egalitarianism are ruled out - historical experience certainly shows that they lead to disaster.

Planning and state control of the financial sector and the monopolies is posed by capitalist development itself. Confiscation could be used as a political weapon against those capitalists who refuse to cooperate or who rebel. But the full socialisation of production is dependent on and can only proceed in line with the withering away of skills monopolies of the middle class and hence the division of labour.

The economy under working class rule will therefore be contradictory: there is a socialised part and a part which consists of surviving capitalist elements. The aim, however, is to slowly extend the socialised part of the economy so as to finally replace the market and the law of value with conscious planning and production for human need. Socialism will thereby transform the commodity back into a product and make labour directly social.

In order to facilitate this we envisage the following measures:

● The radical extension of democratic decision-making in the socialised sector of the economy. Managers to be elected and rotated through short terms of office. All important decisions relating to production, hiring and firing, etc, must be ratified by workers' committees.

● Shorter working hours and a major expansion of adult education and training to facilitate individuals changing jobs and taking on management and coordination roles.

● In the remaining capitalist sector workers will be guaranteed full rights.

● Unemployment will be abolished. There will be an

obligation for everyone to work - the only exception being those who are unable to do so for reasons of health or age.

• Planning must be based on the widest participation, discussion and decision-making processes.

• Production to be redirected towards socially useful ends and to be reorganised so as to radically reduce the major social and international economic inequalities.

• Limited liability and corporate personality will be abolished. Tax loopholes will be closed and inheritance tax made genuinely progressive.

• Tax and other measures to encourage cooperatives.

5 Transition to Communism

Socialism is not a mode of production. It is the transition from capitalism to communism. Socialism is communism which emerges from capitalist society. It begins as capitalism with a workers' state. Socialism therefore bears the moral, economic and intellectual imprint of capitalism.

In general, socialism is defined as the rule of the working class.

The division of labour cannot be abolished overnight. It manifests itself under socialism in the contradictions between mental and manual labour, town and country, men and women, as well as social, regional and national differences.

Classes and social strata exist under socialism because of different positions occupied in relationship to the means of production, the roles played in society and the way they receive their income.

Class and social contradictions necessitate the continuation of the class struggle. However, this struggle is reshaped by the overthrow of the capitalist state and the transition towards communism.

The class struggle can, in the last analysis, go in two directions, depending on the global balance of forces. It can go backwards or it can advance towards communism.

While socialism creates the objective basis for solving social contradictions, these contradictions need to be solved through a correct political line and the development of mass, active democracy. This is essential, as communism is not a spontaneous development.

Social strata will only finally disappear with full communism.

5.1 The socialist state

In its first stages communism has not reached complete maturity or completely rid itself of the traditions and remnants of capitalism. The class struggle and private property continue and so does the need for the state.

The socialist state (the rule of the working class or proletarian dictatorship) is needed in the first place to counter capitalist resistance. Though this can involve draconian measures, it must be emphasised that as the rule of a large majority the socialist state is characterised by the fullest flowering of democracy. The socialist state dispenses with much of the bureaucratic and military baggage of the capitalist state - it is a semi-state.

The repressive role of the state is not only connected with overcoming the capitalist class. There is also the division of labour. Until work becomes life's prime want, laws, courts and state coercion will be required.

The global rule of the working class will make it possible for the state to begin to disappear in its entirety, as classes wither away on the basis of the socialisation of the productive forces on a global scale.

5.2 Socialism and democracy

Socialism and democracy are inseparable. The rule by the majority is in the first place attained by the truly mass, truly democratic breaking apart of the bourgeois state and its replacement by the extreme democracy of the working class.

To begin with, certain functions of the state and administration remain a sphere of specialists. Our aim is not rule by a stratum of specialists (that is, bureaucracy - an alienated form of organisation) in the name of the majority. Rather rule by the majority itself. The extension of democracy against bureaucracy is therefore a principal form of class struggle.

Socialism must progressively involve the entire population in administration and management. Democracy is not only the casting of votes. It is a process of the constant forming of ideas, and taking and carrying out decisions. Hence the need for democratic control over every sphere of life: the state and politics, work and economy, international relations.

Without open discussion as a norm and allowing for the formation of platforms and oppositions for the presentation of different views, democracy can only be formal.

5.3 Communism

Socialism in the 21st century will start from a relatively high level of technique, output and culture. Once the hard task of winning working class state power has been achieved, we will advance towards full communism. The speed of that advance is dictated by the completion of the world revolution and the correctness of the policy of the working class and its party.

Through society reabsorbing the functions of the state the need for it withers away. Democracy (as a form of the state) negates itself and gives way to general freedom. The higher stage of communism is a free association of producers. Everybody will contribute according to their ability and take according to their need. Real human history begins and society leaves behind the realm of necessity. In the realm of freedom people will become rounded, fully social individuals, who can for the first time truly develop their natural humanity.

This is what we want to achieve. To win that prize we shall overcome all obstacles.

6 The Communist Party

The Communist Party of Great Britain is the voluntary union of communists. It is guided by the theory established by Karl Marx and Friedrich Engels and organised according to the principles of democratic centralism.

The Communist Party is the highest form of class organisation of the proletariat. The Communist Party is a class party, the advanced part of the working class. The Communist Party is formed and built by the self-selection of the most dedicated, most courageous and most far-sighted workers. Because of this it can fulfil the role of the theoretical, political and organisational vanguard of the proletariat.

The Communist Party has no interest other than that of the proletariat as a whole. The Communist Party differs from the rest of the working class only in that it has the advantage of a theory which enables it to understand the historical path and results of proletarian class struggle. Hence at every stage and turn of events it champions the general interests of the movement.

Consequently, as advanced workers and true partisans of the working class, the communists understand the necessity of coming together in the CPGB.

6.1 Party of all workers

Communists always support the organisation of the working class in the largest, most powerful and most centralised units.

In the absence of objective conditions compelling separate organisation, the proletariat organises as a single party. This is a requirement of proletarian internationalism.

The vanguard of the working class organises in a single party based on the existing borders of the bourgeois state that is to be overthrown. Those who fail to fight for such organisational unity of the workers have not broken their links with nationalism.

Objective conditions in Britain require the workers of all nationalities to organise in a single Communist Party.

6.2 CPGB is internationalist

The CPGB stands on the principles of proletarian internationalism. It is a proletarian-internationalist duty for communists to make revolution in their own country. However, the struggle for socialism in Britain is subordinated to the struggle for world revolution. Proletarian internationalism renders it compulsory for the interests of the workers' struggle in one country to be subordinated to the interests of that struggle on a world scale.

Understanding the unity of the interests and aims of the world working class does not arise spontaneously within the national workers' movement. The CPGB has to conscientiously imbue the working class struggle with the ideas of proletarian internationalism and uncompromisingly fight against nationalism. The CPGB sees it as its duty to fight against any trend which harms the unity of the world's working class around communism. We are well aware of the connection between nationalism and opportunism and revisionism.

The CPGB believes that the world proletariat needs a world strategy and world organisation. Without a world communist party the working class is weakened and lacks coordination. The CPGB will do all in its power to rectify this situation.

6.3 Principles of organisation

The foremost and unchanging task of communists is to conduct systematic, all-sided and principled agitation and propaganda. In our conditions this means combating all manifestations of bourgeois ideology and winning the masses to the idea of revolution.

6.3.1 Central publication

The party conducts propaganda and agitation on the basis of its central publication. The central publication is not only a collective propagandist and collective agitator. It is also a collective organiser.

Organisation around the distribution network of the central publication and education on the basis of the central publication constitute the basis for the continuous action of our party.

6.3.2 The basic unit

The basic organisational unit of the Communist Party is the cell. The cell is the only unit of the party in which all members must participate. Established on the basis of task, workplace or locality, the basic unit facilitates the closest and broadest relations with the masses.

Cells have autonomy within their sphere of responsibility and should be self-sustaining and constantly striving to take initiatives. Cells work to train their members as professional revolutionaries who have educated themselves, learnt the skills of the revolutionary struggle and dedicated their whole life to the cause.

6.3.3 Criticism and self-criticism

Criticism and self-criticism, including in public, on an individual and collective level are the first condition for the unity, development and growth of the Communist Party. The aim is to continually strengthen the party's ability to serve the working class and humanity.

Criticism in no way implies the undermining of the individual or collective concerned, but improving their contribution to the party and party discipline. It shows the individual or collective being criticised why their attitude accords with neither the interests of the class nor the party.

Bourgeois and petty bourgeois influences constantly manifest themselves in the party. The party too lives in a world dominated by the spontaneously generated ideas of capitalism. Hence if the mistakes of individuals or collectives are not corrected they can become a deviation or even embedded amongst the majority of members. Criticism and self-criticism is one of the most effective weapons against such dangers.

6.3.4 Men and women

There must be no discrimination between men and women in the Communist Party. Male communists must practise equality and female communists must insist on it.

However, given the male-dominated culture we operate in and the need to win women to follow the lead and join the ranks of the Communist Party, every effort should be made to promote women comrades in the party. In this way, the party develops its culture and extends its strength for the struggle.

6.3.5 Legality and illegality

Communists make no mechanical division between legality and illegality under the conditions of bourgeois rule. They are not opposites, but different moments in the development of the class struggle.

Democratic rights under capitalism are not granted by the generosity of the ruling class. Nor are they inherent in the system. They have been won by struggle in the face of fierce opposition by generation after generation of working people.

The scope of legal work is determined by the balance of forces between the ruling and working class. Even when bourgeois rule is masked in a democratic form, state terror is always held in reserve.

The Communist Party therefore - even in the most democratic of periods - maintains and endeavours to constantly improve its illegal work. Our party must be a combat organisation of the working class.

Thus, we do not build an illegal apparatus for its own

sake. We do it to win the freedom to make revolution, an act that no bourgeois state tolerates. A Communist Party is only as free as the struggle it wages for revolution is free from the restrictions of bourgeois legality.

The ultimate guarantee of the freedom of the party to make revolution is the correctness of its scientific world view and its ability to merge with the broad masses of the class. We guard against state provocation and infiltration primarily through the open fight for correct politics.

6.3.6 Leadership

If the working class is to defeat the bourgeoisie, it must train leaders from among its ranks who are not inferior to those of the bourgeoisie. No class can function without leaders. Even anarchist groups have leaders, though they are often autocratic, hidden and unaccountable.

Instead of promoting personality cults communists emphasise committees and collective responsibility. We seek to demystify and democratise leadership through open debate, regular elections, recallability and actively promoting the aim of making all members into potential leaders - judged by theoretical knowledge, revolutionary energy and political instinct and experience. That allows individuals to be easily replaced, enhances institutional continuity and provides the means for members to correct errors: that is, to lead.

6.3.7 No ready-made blueprints

The CPGB applies the Leninist principle of organisation. There are no ready-made blueprints for communist organisation. Timeless recipes for the structure and relationship between the various bodies that make up the Communist Party are the result of formal, not dialectical, thinking.

We proceed from the fact that the Communist Party is a living organism. It evolves and constantly changes according to objective circumstances and the struggle to put the revolutionary programme into practice. The CPGB will therefore constantly modify itself organisationally.

6.3.8 CPGB is democratic centralist

The CPGB is organised on the basis of democratic centralism. Democratic centralism is a form of organisation and a political principle.

Democratic centralism entails the subordination of the minority to the majority when it comes to the actions of the party. That does not mean that the minority should be gagged. Minorities must have the possibility of becoming the majority. As long as they accept in practice the decisions of the majority, groups of comrades have the right to support alternative platforms and form themselves into temporary or permanent factions and express their views publicly.

Democratic centralism therefore represents a dialectical unity entailing the fullest, most open and frank debate, along with the most determined, selfless, revolutionary action.

Democratic centralism allows the members of the Communist Party to unitedly carry out actions, elect and be elected, criticise the mistakes of the party and self-criticise their own failings without fear or favour. In essence then, democratic centralism is a process whereby communists are united around correct aims and principles.

6.3.9 Communist discipline

Party discipline consists of the duty to voice differences, complete fulfilment of assigned tasks and not withholding financial resources.

Communist discipline develops on the basis of positively resolving differences and successfully developing ties with the masses. Mutual respect and the strength of the working class increases the level of communist discipline.

6.4 Communists and trade unions

Trade unions are basic organisations of working class defence. The Communist Party is the highest form of working class organisation. The party and the trade unions are therefore different organisations of the same class.

Communists do not seek to blur the different roles of the party and the trade unions. When trade unionists attempt to assume the functions of the Communist Party, they weaken the trade unions and the party. When the Communist Party attempts to assume the functions of the trade unions, it likewise weakens the trade unions and the party.

Communists defend the organisational independence of the unions, but seek to win them to accept the political leadership of the Communist Party.

Communists fight for internal democracy in the unions and against all forms of bureaucracy.

Communists are confident that sooner or later the trade unions will be won to their views and be made into schools for communism. Communists put forward a consistent perspective which unites, not divides, the trade unions. Communists fight both sectionalism and splits along economic or political lines in the trade union movement and bring to the fore the common interest. In this way, communists show that they are the best fighters for the day-to-day interests of the proletariat, as well as those who look after the interests of the future.

Communists tirelessly work in the trade unions to fight bourgeois ideology. We explain that no trade union demand can be made permanent while wage-slavery lasts. All economic, trade union and political demands must be connected with the task of putting society as a whole into the hands of the working class.

6.5 Communists and religion

The Communist Party says that the state should consider religion a private matter. However, from the point of view of the party itself, religion - whether it be an established cult or a residual belief in the supernatural - is not a private matter. Our party cannot be indifferent to the ignorance, gullibility and irrationality religion engenders in the minds of the masses. The CPGB therefore conducts atheist propaganda.

Unless the working class is educated through its own struggle against capitalism, atheist propaganda will only have limited effect. That is why the CPGB leads the struggle of the masses against every form of capitalist ideology and connects its atheist propaganda to the class struggle against capitalism and its state.

The holding of individual religious belief is no obstacle to membership of the CPGB. All religious people who are committed to the cause of the working class and the liberation of humanity should join the communists.

Draft rules

The Communist Party of Great Britain was founded on July 31 1920 as a militant vanguard. It united in its ranks the most politically conscious, most courageous, most organised section of the workers' movement. That made the CPGB the advanced part of the proletariat in Britain.

In its early years our party undoubtedly suffered from a certain amateurishness and economism. This was a carry-over from the past. Despite that, because of its revolutionary political and organisational principles, the party was able to take a lead in all the great struggles of the day and considerably deepen and widen its influence amongst the masses.

However, by the late 1920s signs of opportunist decay were all too evident. No doubt with the best subjective intentions many of our leaders began to see themselves as an extension of the Soviet Union's foreign policy.

To serve these ends the leadership as a whole was congealed into a faction and, citing democratic centralism as justification, it began treating the party as its own property.

The claim to be operating democratic centralism was, of course, no longer true. What the leadership was concerned with was not revolutionary clarity, but silencing opposition. Democratic centralism had become bureaucratic centralism.

Things follow their own logic. What began as persecution in the name of the monolithic party ended as the liquidation of the party.

In the 1970s the Eurocommunist Marxism Today faction emerged from within the leadership. By the 1980s, craving respectability in the eyes of bourgeois society, it determinedly set about liquidating the party organisationally.

Minorities, above all the Leninist minority, were barred from 'official' party publications. Instead, these were given over to liberals, churchmen, police chiefs and reactionaries of all hues. Minorities had no possibility of becoming the majority. Not only were the various opposition trends denied places on leading committees: they were subject to crude bans and expulsions.

The open, disciplined and principled rebellion by Leninists was an important turning point in the life of the party. It was a rebellion against the bureaucratic centralist regime of the Marxism Today faction. It was also a rebellion against the entire history of opportunism in our party.

It was understood that the party had to be reforged. That meant a new revolutionary programme and new party rules which were actually based on democratic centralism.

These rules have been prepared with the aim of securing the necessary centralism and democracy of the CPGB, if it is to organise around its programme and put it into practice.

1 Aim
Article 1. The aim of the Communist Party of Great Britain is the voluntary union of communists, the overthrow of the capitalist state, the establishment of socialism and the triumph of communism.

2 Membership
Article 2. A member is one who joins the party, accepting its rules and programme, works in a party organisation and regularly pays dues.

Article 3. Except in exceptional circumstances application for membership is submitted individually. An applicant must be recommended by a party body. Application is subject to the approval by the next higher body. The proposing body must supply reliable information on the member being accepted.

Article 4. Party members are required to fulfil all tasks assigned to them by the party, to fight for the party's unity in action and use the party's material resources in a responsible manner. Party members also have a right and a duty to study Marxism and develop the party's political positions.

3 Organisation of Party life

Article 5. The organisational principles of the party are based on democratic centralism. The part is subordinate to the whole, lower committees to higher, all committees to the Central Committee and the Central Committee to the congress.

Article 6. Except where the rules state otherwise, in all party bodies decisions are taken by the majority of members participating in the meeting. It is the right and the duty of party members to participate in the meetings of the bodies of which they are a member and to openly state their views on all matters concerning the party. In between meetings the tasks assigned by the secretary must be fulfilled.

Article 7. Party bodies are established on the basis of task, locality or workplace. Within their sphere of responsibility they are autonomous.

Article 8. Higher committees have the right to appoint representatives to participate in the meetings of lower bodies and establish relations with their members.

Article 9. During a particular action members have the right to submit their views to higher committees up to the Central Committee for discussion and to the central publication for publication. While acting fully in accordance with the principle of unity in action, members can oppose decisions taken by higher committees. That includes the right to form factions organised with a view to changing party policy or its leadership.

4 Structure of the Party

Article 10. The basic organisational form of the party is the cell. Cells should be kept as small as possible to allow maximum flexibility and maximum efficiency. Cells should as a norm meet weekly.

Article 11. The Central Committee, or a group of cells in an area, city, district or region, may establish area or city committees, which are responsible for directing the work of at least two cells, or district or regional committees, which are responsible for the work of two or more areas or cities in the district or region.

Article 12. The congress is the highest decision-making body of the party. The congress should normally be held every year. The congress should be announced by the Central Committee at least three months in advance. The congress can be delayed by decision of the Central Committee, but the period between congresses should not exceed two years.

Article 13. Extraordinary congresses can be called by a majority decision of the Central Committee. If more than a third of the membership demand it, the Central Committee is obliged to convene an extraordinary congress. It should be held within three months. Failing that, the next highest committees calling for a congress have the duty to set up an organising committee to convene one. Preparation and representation is decided by the committee convening the congress.

Article 14. The Central Committee may invite delegates to the congress who have speaking but not voting rights.

Article 15. Congress hears, discusses and votes upon all reports, resolutions and matters it considers relevant. Through simple majorities it also decides upon the numbers and composition of the Central Committee, changes in the rules and programme, appeals on matters of discipline, etc.

Article 16. The Central Committee is the highest decision-making body between congresses. The Central Committee elects its own officers. If one third of its members so decide, the chair of the Central Committee must convene an extraordinary meeting of the Central Committee.

Article 17. Decisions of the Central Committee are taken by a simple majority of those members participating. The Central Committee has the power to dissolve and re-establish any party body or publication. The Central Committee may co-opt new members who will not have voting rights.

Article 18. Between congresses or at particularly important junctures a conference may be convened by the Central Committee or a majority of district committees. Conference cannot take the place of the congress. It cannot elect the Central Committee nor change the rules and programme.

5 Discipline

Article 19. The following are violations of party discipline: failure to adhere to party rules; violating organisational security; refusal to support an agreed action; concealing by words, conduct or silence one's political or factional relations and activities; behaving in a way that brings discredit to the party.

Article 20. Any committee of the party can vote on a motion of censure against one of its members. The relevant higher committee must be notified. Votes by a committee to suspend or expel a member must be ratified by the Central Committee. A member who is suspended has no membership rights, only duties. The comrade's level of consciousness and experience should always be taken into account.

Article 21. Every member of the party who is subject to disciplinary procedures has the right to appeal to higher bodies of the party, up to and including the congress.

Article 22. The expulsion of a member of the Central Committee must be agreed by a two-thirds majority of its full membership.

6 Dues
Article 23. The Central Committee determines the level of membership dues. Dispensation can be negotiated in particular cases by the basic committees, but have to be ratified by the Central Committee.

7 Party property
Article 24. Party property is held by the relevant officers or trustees of the party in trust for the members of the party subject to the rights and duties created by these rules.

Article 25. In the event of dissolution of the party, party property shall be transferred to another organisation or organisations having aims as similar as possible to those of the party, decided by a majority vote of the members of CPGB.